CHILDREN'S TEA & ETIQUETTE

Brewing Good Manners in Young Minds

Dorothea Johnson, John Harney & Ann Noyes

Illustrated by Dawn Peterson

Recipes by Bruce Richardson

This book is dedicated
to all generations, young and old,
and especially to those wonderful relationships
between grandparents and grandchildren.

Our mission is to inform children
about having and using good manners and
to tell children about tea's ancient roots.

ISBN13 978-0-966347-89-0
ISBN 0-96634-789-7

Child's tea set courtesy of Andrea by Sadek.
Printed in China through Four Colour Imports, Ltd.

Benjamin Press
PO Box 100
Perryville, KY 40468
800.765.2139
www.benjaminpress.com

Welcome!

There is something magical about a tea party that casts a spell on children of all ages. It's a wonderful enchantment that charms anyone who answers the invitation, "Would you like a cup of tea?"

My son, Ben, had his first tea party at age six when we invited his first grade class to join us for a May Day dance and tea. He and his classmates wore their best clothes to class that day. They walked the short distance from school to our front yard where a Maypole with colorful streamers had been placed.

The children danced around the Maypole while our dog, Freckles, howled to the music. Afterwards, the children and their teachers came into our dining room for a morning tea party. "Please" and "thank you" filled the air as the children passed the pots of hot tea and delicious goodies to each other.

The teachers were so surprised to see everyone on their best behavior! I knew they would be. Children always exhibit their finest manners when they come to a tea party. The class enjoyed it so much that they came back the next year, and continued to look forward to the May Day tea parties through all their elementary years. It left them with valuable memories and the confident dining skills they still use today.

Join my friend, Dorothea Johnson, as she uses a tea party as a classroom to teach children classic dining and social manners.

— Bruce Richardson —

The Invitation

Harry and Kate were very excited to see their Gramma and Papa and gave them big hugs as they opened a card inviting them to a tea party.

They were happy to accept the invitation but were curious about the word intergenerational and the abbreviation RSVP. They asked their grandparents to explain those words.

> *Y*ou are invited
> to join us for an
> *Intergenerational Tea Party*
> *Saturday,*
> *the fourteenth of June*
> *in the Botanical Gardens*
>
> *History of Tea at Two o'clock*
>
> *Tea Party at Three o'clock*
>
> *Please wear your best clothes*
>
> *RSVP to 555-1234*

Papa said, "Intergenerational means all ages of moms and dads, grandparents, aunts and uncles, their nieces and nephews, and special friends."

Gramma explained that RSVP is the abbreviation for a French term, *repondez s'il vous plait*, which means, "Please respond." She also added that when you receive an invitation, you should tell the host whether or not you will attend the party.

Who are the members of your intergenerational family?
What is your favorite name for your grandparents?
How do you respond to an invitation?

The First Meeting

Harry and Kate's grandparents enjoy sharing their knowledge about many things and thought it would be fun to talk with them about manners, and also what to expect when they go to the tea party. They asked their friend, Ms. Johnson, if she would meet with the children and give them some lessons in manners and the etiquette of a tea party.

Gramma said, "Ms. Johnson, I'd like to introduce Harry and Kate Goss, our grandchildren." She told the children, "Ms. Johnson is a well-known expert on etiquette, and has helped many people learn good manners."

Harry and Kate knew how to be polite, and stood up as they put out their right hands and took turns shaking hands.

"Hello, Ms. Johnson," they said as they greeted her.

She replied, "Children, it's a delight to meet you. I'm looking forward to spending the afternoon with you talking about manners and tea. Let's get started!"

Shaking Hands

It's important to shake hands when you meet another person. Reach out your right hand, fingers straight out and together, thumb up, and let the palm of your hand meet the palm of the other person's hand. Give a gentle squeeze with one or two shakes of the hand. That makes a great handshake!

Introducing Yourself

When you meet someone for the first time, it's important to say, "Hello, my name is _____." Always say your first and last name.

Smiling and Making Eye Contact

Smile and look into the person's eyes and make eye contact as you say hello.

Sitting In A Chair

There is a correct way to sit in a chair – simply pull the chair out from the table and enter from the right side of the chair.

Picking Up Your Napkin

Always wait for the host or older person to pick up his or her napkin before you pick up yours. Now you may pick up your napkin and place it on your lap; then open it with the crease towards your waist.

Drinking A Cup Of Tea

After the tea has been poured, you may add sugar, and/or milk. Lemon should not be used with milk.

Please Pass the Jam

When there is something on the table that you can't reach, simply say, "Please pass the jam, milk or sugar."

Eating Tea Sandwiches, Scones and Desserts

The first food served at a tea party will be a delicious selection of little sandwiches (also called "savories"), which may be picked up with your fingers. These are eaten first.

Scones usually are served next, accompanied by jam and clotted cream. If you would like to enjoy a bite-sized piece of the scone, slice through the scone while it is resting on your plate. Break off a small piece with your fingers and use your knife to spread some jam, then clotted cream and put it in your mouth.

If you prefer a larger portion, slice the scone in half length-wise while it is resting on your plate. Lift off the top piece and place it on your plate (now you have two pieces of scone). Using your knife, first spread the bottom half with jam followed by clotted cream. Now take a bite.

Once you finish the bottom half of the scone, you may spread the jam and clotted cream on the top piece and enjoy its crumbly texture and flavor. Be ready to use your napkin if you get some jam or cream around your mouth.

Desserts are eaten last. Cookies may be picked up with the fingers, but a fork is used to eat other desserts, such as cake.

Remember: this is a time to share and take only one from each selection so that everyone has a bite of each tasty treat!

Leaving The Table

When you are leaving the table for a brief time and will be returning, always say, "Please excuse me." Exit the chair from the right side, place the napkin on the chair seat and push the chair under the table.

When you are leaving the table at the end of tea, place the napkin to the left side of the plate, exit the chair from the right side and push the chair under the table.

Magic Words

Tea parties are places for your best manners. Ms. Johnson asked Harry and Kate to tell her some of the "magic words" they use to show they are polite and have good manners.

Together, Harry and Kate thought of these magic words:

"Please." "Thank You." "May I?" "You're Welcome."

Ms. Johnson could see that Harry and Kate thought all the manner lessons were a lot to remember, but they thanked her and promised they would try very hard to use their best manners and magic words at the tea party.

Do you stand and shake hands when you meet someone?
Do you call an adult by a grown-up title such as Mr., Ms., or Mrs.?
When have you used your best manners and "magic words"?

The Tea Party Day

Finally, the day came for the tea party. Harry wore his new navy blue blazer and grey slacks, and Kate wore her pink party dress.

They were so excited and kept looking out the window as they waited for their grandparents. Finally, they arrived!

Papa had a big smile on his face when he got out of the car. He held the door open for the children. They thanked him as they entered and sat next to Gramma. And off they went!

When they arrived at the Botanical Gardens, there was a huge colorful banner that had "Intergenerational Tea Party" written on it. They could see colorful balloons everywhere, and there were tables and chairs placed among the flower gardens.

As they walked through the gate, they saw a yellow and white striped tent with colorful silk ribbons waving in the breeze and a sign that read:

> ### History of Tea
> **John Harney, speaker**
> *Two o'clock*

Harry and Kate's grandparents said, "Before we attend the tea party, we are going to learn about the history of tea from our friend John Harney, a well-known tea blender."

Where do you think tea grows? How is it made?

History of Tea

They entered the tent and found four seats very close to the front and sat down. Mr. Harney and Ms. Johnson were standing near them, surrounded by photographs, a tea map, posters, teapots and tea samples. They could see Mr. Harney's friendly smile and twinkling eyes as he was introduced.

"Good afternoon, and welcome to my favorite subject, the History of Tea. My name is John Harney, and I am going to tell you a story about how tea may have been discovered. Please pretend the year is 2737 B.C. and you are the Emperor of China. Your name is Shen Nung.

"You are sitting under a wild tea tree. The breeze has stirred the leaves of the tree and a few of them have fallen into a pot of water you are boiling. You taste the liquid and find it delicious – and that's how tea may have been discovered. We know the enjoyment of tea began in China, then moved to Europe, England, the United States, and nearly every country in the world.

"Please look at this photograph. The beautiful bush with shiny green leaves and small creamy blossoms with a yellow center," Mr. Harney continued, "is called *Camellia sinensis*— and all tea comes from this particular bush.

"Usually only the new shoots (the new growth of the top two leaves and leaf bud) are handpicked from the bush. After the

leaves are picked they become either green, oolong, or black teas through a drying, steaming, and oxidation process." Mr. Harney then asked the children, "How long do you think it takes to pick enough tea to fill a basket?"

After many guesses he said, "Those are great answers, but it takes about three to three and one-half hours to fill a basket with the smaller tea leaves, and two hours for the larger tea leaves. So, now you can understand why tea is so special and a treat for us to drink.

"Let's look at the World Tea Map and some of the countries where tea is grown."

Why do you think there is no tea grown in Canada, Denmark or Iceland?

Countries Where Tea is Grown

Argentina, Australia, Azerbaijan, Azores, Bangladesh, Brazil, Burundi, Cameroon, China, Ecuador, Ethiopia, Georgia, India, Indonesia, Iran, Japan, Kenya, Madagascar, Malawi, Malaysia, Mauritius, Mozambique, Nepal, Papua New Guinea, Peru, Russia, Rwanda, South Africa, Sri Lanka, Tanzania, Turkey, Uganda, United States, Vietnam, Zimbabwe

---

Some Different Names of Tea

Assam, Bancha, Darjeeling, Earl Grey, English Breakfast,
Gunpowder, Gyokuro, Irish Breakfast, Jasmine,
Lapsang Souchong, Oolong, Orange Pekoe, Sencha

"Some 'teas' are actually infusions and do not come from the tea plant, *Camellia sinensis*, but from herbs, fruits, and flowers. They do not contain caffeine," Mr. Harney said.

"I thank everyone for joining me to learn about the earliest history of tea. Now, I invite you to join me for a cup of tea."

The audience applauded as Ms. Johnson thanked Mr. Harney for his informative talk about the history of tea.

The Intergenerational Tea Party

Mr. Harney and Ms. Johnson joined Harry and Kate and their grandparents as they went to their table. Harry and Kate said hello to their friends from school and introduced them to everyone at their table.

The tables were beautifully set with pretty tablecloths and napkins, tiered trays of food, and pots of steaming tea.

The Intergenerational Tea Party

Menu

Mayflower Tea Sandwiches
Cucumber Tea Sandwiches
Cheddar Cheese Wafers
Savory Tartlets

Scones with Mock Devonshire Cream
and Strawberry Jam

Double Dipped Strawberries
Lemon Bars
Fruited Oatmeal Tea Cakes
Shortbread Hearts
Brownie Tea Cakes

Orange Coconut Sorbet

Assortment of Teas

The food was delicious, and everyone had a wonderful time talking, laughing, enjoying the day and a special time together – and using their very best tea manners.

When the tea party ended, Harry and Kate thanked Mr. Harney and Ms. Johnson. They then turned to their grandparents and thanked them for a very special day.

Driving home with Gramma and Papa, Harry and Kate knew they would always remember this wonderful day.

Writing a Thank You Note

The next morning, they awoke very early. After eating breakfast, Harry and Kate sat down to write Gramma and Papa a thank you note even though they had already said "thank you" in person.

Dear Gramma and Papa,

Thank you for our best manners class with Ms. Johnson, the history of tea lesson with Mr. Harney, and the delicious and fun tea party.

We think you are the best grand-parents in the whole-wide world.

Lots of hugs and kisses,

Harry and Kate

For Grown-ups:

The Correct Way to Brew Tea

1. Preheat a teapot by pouring boiling water into it, raising the temperature of the pot to 190° F.

2. Discard the water. For a teapot holding up to 6 cups, add one teaspoon of loose tea for each cup you are brewing. For pots that hold up to 12 cups, add an extra teaspoon of tea "for the pot." If you are using a teabag, use one teabag per cup.

3. Pour fresh boiling water over the tea or teabag. This super-saturates the tea, allowing the perfect extraction of flavor.

4. Black Tea and Infusions: The water temperature should be 212° F. Steep for four to five minutes.

5. Green Tea: The water temperature should be below the boiling point, about 180° F. Steep for three minutes.

6. If using loose tea, pour tea through a strainer into a cup. If using a teabag, remove teabag from pot or cup.

For Everyone:

Hints and Tips

- Do take small bites.

- Do talk in a quiet voice.

- Do put sugar, milk, or lemon in the cup after the tea has been poured, not before.

- Do place the spoon on the saucer, not on the table.

- Do sip your tea and no slurping!

- Do use your napkin.

- Don't talk with food in your mouth.

- Don't put your elbows on the table.

- Don't push your plate away when you are finished eating.

- Write a thank you note to the person who invited you.

Can you think of some other helpful hints and tips for the list?

RECIPES

Mayflower Tea Sandwiches

1 8-oz package cream cheese
1/4 cup orange marmalade
1/4 teaspoon almond extract
25 pieces white bread, cut into 2-inch rounds
1 small package slivered almonds
25 large wild violet leaves, washed (optional)
yellow food coloring

Using an electric mixer, mix together the cream cheese, marmalade, and almond extract until smooth. Flatten each piece of bread with a rolling pin and spread with enough cheese mixture to just cover the bread. Pinch together 1/3 of the round to make a cone.

Coat almonds with yellow food coloring and place one sliver into the throat of each bread cone. Place the assembled flower on a wild violet leaf and serve.

Cucumber Tea Sandwiches

16 slices of cracked wheat bread
1/2 cup butter, softened
2 tablespoons chopped fresh chives
2 tablespoons chopped fresh parsley
2 teaspoons lemon juice
1 medium cucumber, thinly sliced
carrot curls

Remove crust from bread and cut into rounds. In a small bowl, combine butter, chives, parsley, and lemon juice. Blend well. Spread each bread round with herb butter mixture. Top with a cucumber slice and garnish with a carrot curl.

RECIPES

Savory Tartlets

Short Crust Pastry

2 cups flour
Pinch of salt
1/2 cup cold butter
1 egg yolk
1 teaspoon lemon juice
2 tablespoons ice water

Sift flour and salt into a medium bowl. Cut in butter with a pastry blender until mixture resembles coarse crumbs. In a small bowl, whisk together egg yolk and lemon juice. Pour this into flour mixture and add enough ice water to give dough the consistency needed. Turn dough onto a floured surface and knead lightly. Wrap in plastic wrap and refrigerate for 30 minutes before using.

Preheat oven to 375° F. Grease 12 2-inch tartlet pans. Roll out pastry on a floured surface. Cut 12 rounds with a 2 1/2" cookie cutter. Line each tartlet pan with a pastry round. (Frozen tart shells may be used, if desired.)

Filling

3/4 cup grated sharp cheddar cheese
1 egg
1/2 cup milk
salt and pepper to taste
parsley, oregano and basil (fresh or dried), finely chopped

Sprinkle each pastry round with 1 tablespoon of cheese. Whisk together egg, milk, salt, and pepper. Pour into pastry shells and sprinkle with herbs. Bake 35-40 minutes or until pastry is golden and filling is set.

Scones

2 cups all-purpose flour
2 teaspoons baking powder
1/2 teaspoon salt
1/4 teaspoon baking soda
6 tablespoons unsalted cold butter
1/2 cup currants (optional)
1/2 cup buttermilk
1 egg
1 tablespoon cream
1 tablespoon sugar

Preheat oven to 400° F. Lightly grease a large baking sheet. Combine flour, baking powder, salt, and soda. With a pastry blender, cut in butter, mixing until mixture resembles coarse crumbs. Mix in currants if desired.

In a small bowl, whisk buttermilk and egg together, then add to flour mixture. Stir together until a soft ball of dough forms. Turn onto a lightly floured surface and knead gently, turning five or six times.

Roll out dough with a floured rolling pin to about 1/2" thickness. Using a biscuit cutter, cut scones out and place on baking sheet. Brush tops lightly with cream and sprinkle with sugar. Bake 10-12 minutes or until light brown. Serve warm.

RECIPES

Mock Devonshire Cream

1 cup heavy whipping cream
1/2 cup powdered sugar
1 1/2 teaspoons white vanilla extract
1 8-oz carton sour cream

Beat whipping cream, sugar, and vanilla until stiff. Fold sour cream into this mixture and refrigerate. Serve with warm scones.

Double-Dipped Strawberries

36 large fresh strawberries
1 1/2 cups semi-sweet chocolate chips
1 1/2 cups chocolate sprinkles

Rinse strawberries and pat dry. Line a baking sheet with waxed paper. Melt chocolate in a double-boiler over simmering water until mixture is smooth. (If chocolate needs extra smoothness, add about 1 tablespoon of cream.)

Hold individual strawberries by the crown and dip small end of berry into chocolate. Place berries on waxed paper. Scatter sprinkles on berries while chocolate is wet. Refrigerate at least one hour before serving.

RECIPES

Lemon Bars

1 1/2 cups unbleached all-purpose flour
1 teaspoon baking powder
1/2 teaspoon salt
1 15-oz can sweetened condensed milk
1/4 teaspoon lemon oil
1/2 cup lemon juice
1 1/2 sticks butter
1 cup brown sugar, firmly packed
1 cup old-fashioned or quick cooking oats

Preheat oven to 325° F. Sift together flour, baking powder, and salt. Set aside.

Combine sweetened condensed milk, lemon oil and lemon juice in a medium mixing bowl. Whisk until smooth. Mixture will thicken. Set aside.

In a large bowl, cream butter and sugar. Add the sifted ingredients, then the oats. Mixture will be crumbly. Pat two cups of crumbs into bottom of a greased 9" x 13" pan. Spread condensed milk mixture on crumb layer. Sprinkle remaining crumb mixture over milk layer, smoothing gently.

Bake for 30-35 minutes or until brown around edges. Remove pan from oven and cool completely before cutting. Refrigerate, but let come to room temperature before serving.

Shortbread Hearts

2 cups unsalted butter
1 cup granulated sugar
1 teaspoon almond extract
dash of salt
4 cups all-purpose flour
1 cup finely chopped almonds
1 cup powdered sugar
red food coloring (optional)

Preheat oven to 325° F. In a large bowl, beat granulated sugar and butter until fluffy. Add almond extract and a dash of salt. Beat well. Add flour and stir until well mixed. Stir in almonds. Roll out on a floured surface to 1/4" thickness. Cut with any size heart-shaped cookie cutter.

Place the cookies on an ungreased cookie sheet and bake for 15-20 minutes. Cookies should not brown. Cool on wire rack.

Mix together 1 cup powdered sugar and just enough warm water to make a spreadable icing. If desired, tint pink with 1 drop of red food coloring. Spread icing on cookies.

RECIPES

Brownie Tea Cakes

3/4 cup butter
1 ounce semi-sweet chocolate
1 ounce unsweetened chocolate
1 3/4 cups sugar
4 eggs
1 teaspoon vanilla extract
1 cup all-purpose flour
2 tablespoons cocoa
1/8 teaspoon salt
1 cup walnuts, toasted and chopped (optional)
powdered sugar

Preheat oven to 350° F. Melt butter and chocolate over low heat. Remove from heat and stir in sugar. Add eggs, one at a time, stirring well with each addition. Add vanilla.

Combine flour, cocoa, and salt. Add this to the chocolate mixture. Whisk until smooth. Stir in chopped walnuts.

Spoon batter into paper-lined muffin pans, filling 3/4 full. Bake for 12-15 minutes. Cool and dust with powdered sugar.

Fruited Oatmeal Tea Cakes

1 1/2 cups old-fashioned rolled oats
1 cup flour
3/4 teaspoon salt
1/2 teaspoon baking soda
1/4 teaspoon ground cinnamon
1/2 lb unsalted butter, room temperature
1 cup sugar
1 teaspoon vanilla
1 egg
1/3 cup raisins
1/3 cup chopped dates
1/3 cup chopped dried apricots

Preheat oven to 325° F. Butter a 13" x 9" baking pan. Combine oats, flour, salt, soda, and cinnamon. In another bowl, beat butter, sugar and vanilla until light and fluffy. Beat in egg. Beat in oat mixture just until combined. Fold in fruit.

Spread evenly in baking pan and bake until golden brown (35-40 minutes). Cool completely and cut into squares or triangles.

RECICPES

Orange Coconut Sorbet

2 quarts freshly squeezed orange juice
1 cup simple syrup
1/2 cup cream of coconut
1/2 cup coconut

Mix all ingredients in a large bowl. Freeze in a sorbet maker or in the freezer by pouring mixture into an aluminum bowl and stirring at intervals until firm.

Simple Syrup: In a large sauce pan, combine 1 cup sugar and 1 cup water. Bring to a boil while stirring. Refrigerate until ready to use.

Cheddar Cheese Wafers

2 cups sharp cheddar cheese, shredded
2 cups self-rising flour
2 cups crispy rice cereal
2 sticks butter, softened
1 teaspoon salt
1/2 teaspoon red pepper

Mix all ingredients by hand in a large bowl. Roll into small balls. Place on un-greased cookie sheet and flatten each with a fork. Bake at 350° F for 10 minutes.

INDEX

Recipes courtesy of
Bruce & Shelley Richardson
Taken from:
A Year of Teas at Elmwood Inn
A Tea for All Seasons
The Tea Table

Available from Benjamin Press